INTRODUCTION

Beginning its evolutionary path when the great dinosaurs roamed our planet, the hedgehog is an example of one of the "living fossils" on earth. It has changed very little over many thousands of years. Small size, a prickly coat of spines, and a cosmopolitan insectivorous diet have enabled it to survive and prosper when many other mammals have joined the ranks of the extinct.

pigs as one of the major traditional small mammals from which you can choose. However, its meteoric rise to fame has not been without many problems. Although well documented as a wild species in Europe, little knowledge of its needs, care, and breeding under domestic conditions had been recorded. It happens that the species which has gained popularity as a pet is

Atelerix Albiventris, also called the African pygmy, or white-bellied, hedgehog.

Since the late 1980s, there has been a revival of interest in what are called exotic mammalian pocket pets. Of these, the hedgehog, in many ways a most unlikely candidate, has forged ahead as by far the most popular. Indeed, it seems very likely tha[t] will join the ranks of such pet[s] rabbits, hamsters, and guinea[s]

not European, but rather the African species *Atelerix albiventris*, the so-called pygmy, or white-bellied, hedgehog.

THE RISE TO STARDOM

One of the hedgehog's problems [inter]est in it was as [differ]ent animal [spe]cies which

had its own special husbandry requirements. The fact that its importation from the wild was banned before it really became a major pet resulted in its selling price reaching the $1,000-a-pair level. When this happens, it attracts those whose only desire is to produce as many offspring as possible.

Matters such as correct housing, sound breeding strategy, and in this particular instance, the need to socialize offspring, are relegated to the back burner in favor of housing as many as possible in the smallest of space. Although the hedgehog quickly settled down to become a very prolific breeder, its popularity created a demand greater than the supply. It received a great deal of media attention, which ensured an upbeat market for a couple of years.

Eventually, by 1994, the supply was greater than the demand. The formerly high prices started to fall with a vengeance, which attracted even more breeders to help speed up the downward spiral in its price. Sales outstripped the dispersion of the growing data bank of information on its proper care.

A pair of young hedgehogs. These interesting little pets are continuing to grow in popularity in the world of   small-mammal pets.

A handful of spiny delight!

THE PROBLEMS BEGIN

The folly resulting from the extensive breeding programs of some early investor-breeders soon began to show its effect. Cannibalism, abandonment of young, obesity, aggression, and other undesirable pet traits became increasingly common by 1995 within pet individuals. The situation persists to this day, but through the efforts of the North American Hedgehog Association (NAHA) and many of its dedicated supporter-breeders, things are beginning to change.

It must also be added that TFH Publications, the publisher of this book, has also proved to be a major force. It has helped the hedgehog hobby by its willingness to produce books at various price levels that disperse sound husbandry techniques when other publishers have held back waiting to see how the market grows before they commit to it.

ABOUT THIS BOOK

This book is written for the novice looking for sound practical information on the purchase and care of these delightful little pets. It will also serve as a primer for the staff of pet shops desirous to ensure that they are able to give their customers correct advice on all aspects of management.

The information not only reflects the experiences of the author as a breeder but also those of many of the early pioneer enthusiasts who have been so willing to share their knowledge. Additionally, the author has the benefit of reading the many questions received by the NAHA from concerned owners and breeders—it is hoped that this text will answer these questions where this is possible. If you wish to obtain more detailed information about hedgehogs, you are advised to purchase the larger books on these pets published by TFH, and to subscribe to *Hedgehog World International*, the official glossy magazine of the NAHA. Both sources will ensure that you obtain the maximum amount of information and pleasure from your hedgehog.

A hedgehog that is handled from an early age will make for a good, tractable pet.

VIRTUES & PROBLEMS

One of the most common problems with many pet owners is that they will purchase pets on nothing more than a momentary impulse. Once the novelty of the pet wears off, it is either abandoned to its cage, released into the wild, or passed to a friend. Parents often purchase pets for their children without accepting the responsibility for the pet if the child loses interest it.

animals. By so doing, you can know in advance whether a hedgehog will be a suitable pet for you and your family.

HEDGEHOG VIRTUES

There is no animal that will meet the needs of every pet owner, but the hedgehog has many attributes. This is why it is has "taken off," and its growing popularity is assured, even

Hand-feeding a youngster not only provides sustenance but also builds trust and gentleness.

When a pet is purchased on an impulse, it invariably means that the owner knows little about it, or its needs, when it is taken home. This is especially so with exotic pets and has certainly proved the case with thousands of hedgehogs. Hopefully, you will have purchased this book *before* you purchase one of these

allowing for its potential drawbacks. The drawbacks are more related to its quality of breeding and socialization than to any other factor.

Hedgehogs are very quiet and unobtrusive. They will not annoy your neighbors as might barking dogs or raucous parrots. They have no offensive body odors and

This hedgehog is settling down in his bedding of fresh, clean wood shavings. Hedgehogs are not difficult to care for if you follow the basic principles of good husbandry.

are undemanding in their housing and nutritional needs. Given common sense management, they are hardy and may live up to eight years of age, which is quite good for such a small mammal.

Hedgehogs may not be the most intelligent of critters, but they are curious and active, constantly on the move if given ample room in which to exercise. Being insectivorous, they will happily snack on any bugs, beetles and other insects that may be lurking behind, or under, chairs and other out-of-the-way places that hedgehogs like to explore. Few other pets will render such a service to you!

Like any comparable pet, they will defecate on the floor but will tend to do this at the room perimeters rather than just anywhere, as might house rabbits

Accepting food from a friendly hand is the first step toward developing rapport between pet and owner.

The hedgehog's keen sense of smell enables it to sniff out insects and other live foods.

In sharp contrast with its spines, the African pygmy hedgehog's belly fur is very soft.

or guinea pigs. Nor do they do this anywhere near as often as will the other two pets mentioned.

Most children adore hedgehogs and learn to respect these small animals once they own one.

Once a child has gained the confidence of such a pet, the child will tend not to lose interest so readily in it because he or she has had to work at making the pet friendly, rather than assuming it will automatically be that way.

As general rule, hedgehogs get on well with other popular pets that are larger than themselves, such as dogs and cats, whom they largely ignore, and who do likewise with them once they have experienced the sharp spines. It would be unwise to allow mice, hamsters, or gerbils near a hedgehog, which might attack them.

Hedgehogs are very reliable breeders if housed correctly. The

A hedgehog that is well bred and trusting will not resist being held.

Another virtue of hedgehogs is that they do not mind at all if they are kept as single pets. Nor will they be lonely while you are at work. During that period, they will be asleep and become active at the very time you are around— in the evening. This having been said, they can be "retrained" to be rather more active during daylight hours if required.

"new colors" now being developed are sure to increase interest in breeding for them. NAHA-sanctioned hedgehog shows will become a reality during 1996, and this will further widen the scope for those who enjoy this area of pet ownership.

HEDGEHOG PROBLEMS

If more potential owners would

The hedgehog has a pointy snout and dark brown eyes. It is about the size of a small guinea pig.

seriously consider the problems related to any given pet, there would be far less unhappy animals in our society. If you can accept and cope with the problems, you will have no difficulty with the virtues!

The first thing you must understand about hedgehogs is that when compared to most other pets you might choose from, they are still virtually wild animals. They may well have started on their long journey toward domestication, but they are not there yet.

Any animal that has teeth may, if provoked, use them. Hedgehogs most certainly will. Nor do they always need to be annoyed to do so. Indeed, one of their inherent traits is that they will bite at any scent that proves of interest to them. They are far more likely to bite from this cause than from being fearful, which normally results in their curling into a tight ball.

Biting is *not* a consequence of bad breeding but rather a very natural part of their nature. However, poor breeding will most certainly increase the likelihood they will bite from nervousness. The most important key in avoiding biting potential is to handle the pet daily, allow others to do so, and to try to familiarize the pet with as many scents as possible. What is not novel, or potentially edible, has less interest to the hedgehog, giving it no reason to bite.

This hedgehog is about to begin self-anointing, whereby it will cover the sides of its body with frothy saliva. No one knows the reason for this strange behavior, which is triggered by the hedgehog's encountering a scent that is foreign to it.

A lack of caution will produce painful consequences for this inquisitive canine. Strict supervision is a must for other household pets when they are in the company of a hedgehog.

Given this aspect of their nature, and the sharp spines they possess, the hedgehog is entirely unsuited for children under the age of about eight. Much of course depends on whether the child has been raised in a home where numerous pets have always been kept, and where the parents have taught their children to *always* respect any animal.

Related to their penchant to nip is another possible drawback, but it is very insignificant to most owners. If a hedgehog is given freedom to roam around a carpeted room in which it finds an interesting smell, it may tug on the carpet strands that are carrying the scent. We have had

as many as eight females (at one time) roaming our dining room. We have no visible damage to the carpet, even though one or two hedgehogs have tugged on it.

Another minor drawback with these pets is that they must be protected from low temperatures if hibernation or death is to be avoided. Living in the average home, this will not be a problem; but it could be if you planned to keep them in an outdoor shed where there was no heating during the winter.

The only other drawback to hedgehogs is that they really do need a lot of attention if you want a super little pet. Most other popular pets are very social by nature—dogs, rabbits, rodents, and even cats. Such pets want to be part of a social group. The hedgehog really is not that bothered. This means that you must overcome its solitary tendencies by giving it lots of reasons to enjoy being with you—affection, tidbits, and a lot of handling.

For this reason it is obviously much better to obtain a young individual, or an older one that is already well bonded on humans.

IN CONCLUSION

For some owners, the hedgehog will be the most fascinating pet that they have ever owned. It is very different from any others and has great charm and visual appeal. It is a challenging pet because it does not give its trust as readily as most others; this must be earned by its owner.

A well-socialized hedgehog will allow you to do almost anything with it—and without the risk that it will bite, or suddenly curl into a tight defensive ball. Those unfortunate owners who have obtained poor hedgehogs and wonder how hedgehogs ever became popular have not experienced a really tame hedgehog.

Ponder very carefully all that is discussed in this chapter. If you diligently follow the advice in the rest of the book, the chances are high that you will join the ranks of those for whom these little insectivores are proving to be the ultimate small mammal pet.

Hedgehogs spend a good part of their waking hours foraging for food.

Curled tightly into a ball, this hedgehog exhibits the classic defensive posture.

An albino hedgehog. There is also another white variety that has dark eyes and is known simply as the black-eyed white.

SELECTING A HEDGEHOG

The first and most important advice that you should take when purchasing a hedgehog is: *never* do this until you have established that it is legal in your state or country. If you do purchase a hedgehog and it is illegal, you risk having the pet confiscated and yourself fined.

WHERE TO PURCHASE

Assuming that there are no legal problems, your next decision is where to buy a hedgehog. The source will be very important in minimizing the risk that you will be sold a totally unsuitable pet.

The most important factors to consider when selecting a hedgehog are health and temperament. This specimen exhibits every outward sign of good health.

General guidelines to check for with *any* seller are the following:

1. The premises should be clean, especially the cages in which the hedgehogs are being housed. Cracked food or water containers, food containers that are nearly empty, excessively dirty cage floors, and the absence of nestbox facilities all indicate a seller who is not caring correctly for his stock.

2. If hedgehogs are of selling age and opposite sexes are housed in the same cage, this is very bad management. Many pet owners have obtained youngsters only to find themselves presented with a litter of unwanted babies within two to three weeks of purchasing their pet.

3. If the store assistant cannot tell you the sex of the hedgehog, ask if anyone else working there can. Check the sexes of the stock that is housed together yourself. Again, many pet owners have purchased young "males" only to find that they were females when their litter arrived! It is most unfortunate that such a situation should ever prevail, but it does; and potential owners should know of it to ensure they get exactly what they want.

4. Ask what these pets are fed on. If the seller suggests that they can retain top health on dry cat chow or cottage cheese, he clearly has little knowledge of these pets. Further, it indicates that his supplier's service was inadequate, as does the situations discussed in 2 and 3 above. A good breeder should provide his customers, including the pet shops he sells to, full instructions on diet, general care, sexing, and potential problems.

Likewise, a pet shop that stocks hedgehogs should have found out as much as possible about these pets before they were ever put on sale. Those that do not bring their trade into disrepute, making it harder for the vast majority who provide an excellent service to pet owners.

5. The hedgehog's temperament must be good. When a young hedgehog is first lifted from its cage, it will either remain in a relaxed position, meaning non-defensive, or it will curl into a

A hedgehog that remains relaxed when it is held indicates that the animal is well bonded to humans.

Be sure to check the quality of the spines and make sure that none are missing. Additionally, there should be no bald or reddened areas of skin.

ball. The former is the ideal. This indicates that the pet is very well bonded to humans. However, if it curls into a ball of spines, this is still acceptable behavior as long as it uncurls within a minute. If it remains in a ball, this indicates that it has not been handled very often or is of a very nervous disposition. The first situation just described will improve with regular handling; the second will be a much more difficult proposition. How are you to know which is the case? The answer is you cannot, so it is better to find a youngster that leaves no doubt in your mind that it's a friendly little individual. If you ignore this advice because you are impatient to obtain a hedgehog, you may end up with a very unsuitable pet.

6. Ask if the hedgehog is pedigreed. In itself, this is not any kind of guarantee as to quality, but what it does tell you is that the breeder is enthusiastic enough about

these pets to maintain a record of their ancestry.

All others things being equal, the pedigreed hedgehog is definitely more desirable than one that is not. Its purchase price may be greater than the non-pedigreed pet.

HOW OLD?

Having satisfied yourself as to the credibility of the seller, we can now consider other aspects. These pets are weaned when they are about five to eight weeks of age. This means that the best age to obtain them is when they are at least eight or more weeks old. Weaning is not something that suddenly starts or ends. It is a gradual process that is greatly influenced by the size of the litter and the available foods offered to the youngsters by the breeder.

The better the variety, and the sooner the youngsters are being satiated on solid foods, the less milk or regurgitated foods they will need from their mother. However, even though a weanling may be eating independently, it will still gain benefit from remaining with its mother and siblings for a week or two.

During this period, it will be gaining confidence in moving about without following its mother. If a youngster is taken away from its mother too early, it may become stressed. In this state, it is more likely to succumb to illness than if it is robust and confident.

MALE OR FEMALE?

If your hedgehog is to be a pet, it doesn't matter which sex you obtain. The health and disposition

Hedgehogs can be sexed by examining their underbelly and ano-genital area. This is a male.

Hedgehogs are fascinating, entertaining little creatures that provide endless amusement.

of the individual are the factors that determine suitability. However, if you think you might like two of these animals, the female (sow) is the choice. Two males will eventually start fighting. A male and a female kept together will result in offspring that you may not want. Two or more sows will live happily together and provide company for each other.

COLOR PREFERENCE

At this time, the most commonly seen color pattern is called agouti. Color variants are being established; but, other than the albino, their genetic base, if any, has not yet been determined.

The albino is devoid of pigment, has white spines, pink skin and red eyes. If the eyes are dark, and if there are any pigmented areas on the body, it is not an albino, but a dark or black-eyed white.

The variants include cinnamon, cream, chocolate and bicolors. The last group noted on this list may be sold as polka dot, snowflake, salt and pepper, and a range of other names, none of which have as yet been standardized by the NAHA, which is deliberating on them at the time of this writing. What you should understand is that there is a vast difference between a color pattern that is the result of a genetic mutation and one which is

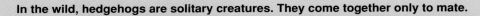

In the wild, hedgehogs are solitary creatures. They come together only to mate.

Members of either sex make equally good pets. This is a female albino.

either environmental, or merely the result of breeder selection for light or darker color individuals that are a natural part of the wild color range.

Bear in mind that the present population of African hedgehogs in the US does contain a number of hybrids, which widens the natural color range. In effect this means, for example, that two so-called cinnamons could mate and not produce the same colored offspring. A number of breeders have advertised given colors that are no more than lighter or darker colored variants on the agouti pattern.

ASSESSING HEALTH

If you have heeded the advice in respect to the source of your hedgehog, you should not have to worry about its health. Even so, you should be aware of how to assess this. You will use this knowledge in your day-to-day observations of the pet.

At once, you will appreciate how important it is that the pet has a good temperament; otherwise, it will be extremely difficult to inspect it if all you can see is a tight ball of spines!

Before giving a physical check, try to watch the pet moving around so that you are satisfied

This mother hedgehog is teaching her young how to forage for food. Logs and fallen trees are good sources of various live foods.

that it shows no signs of limping or other restriction. Hedgehogs can move very quickly. Lameness may be due to a minor sprain, a genetic deficiency, or a permanent or temporary problem with the leg joints. In the case of a temporary problem, the lameness usually clears up after a week or two. However, its exact cause appears not to have been fully established. If apparent at all, it usually appears in youngsters prior to weaning age, so it should not be evident in the stock from which you are choosing. It is best not to take a chance with a lame individual.

The eyes should be round and clear, neither bulging nor sunken.

The ears are small and erect with no signs of scaling. The nose should be dry to just moist, not running. Having said this, it does sometimes happen that a very healthy youngster may have a somewhat wet nose. Why this occurs has yet to be established, other than if a minor chill is present. However, the nose should not be dripping, and the nostrils should not be swollen. All other aspects of the pet should check out as sound.

The anal region should be clean, with no signs of swelling, congealed fecal matter, or staining, which would suggest diarrhea. Carefully inspect the underbelly and facial fur for any

Inspect the underbelly and the anal area, which should not be stained or show any evidence of diarrhea.

A healthy hedgehog will have a dry to just-moist nose and clear, bright eyes with no traces of discharge.

signs of parasites—mites are the most common, especially during hot weather. Also check the base of the spines. It is here that mite action will evidence itself. The spines might also be falling out. There should be no bald and reddened areas of skin, no area of missing spines, or swellings or abrasions anywhere on the body.

If a hedgehog has been kept in a cage with wire bars, for example, a cat carrier, it may be missing a claw or an incisor tooth. This is because it may have been biting on the wire out boredom and frustration with its limited housing space.

There should be five toes on each of the feet, though in the African pygmy hedgehog the rear big toe may be rudimentary or missing.

The final comment on assessing health is that if two or more hedgehogs are sharing the same housing, it is prudent to check the health of each individual in the cage. If any indicate signs of illness, the chances are fair to good that the one you have selected will contract the problem, having been exposed to it.

Food should be served in sturdy, non-tippable bowls. Pet shops carry a wide variety of feeding utensils that are suitable for small mammals such as hedgehogs.

FEEDING

Although the hedgehog is a member of the zoological order known as Insectivora, it is better regarded as being omnivorous in its dietary needs. The name of its zoological order implies a diet almost exclusively of insects and invertebrates, but omnivores take a much wider range of foods, including those of both plant and animal origins. This is especially so under captive conditions, in which you are not able to duplicate the wild diet and therefore need to substitute foods of corresponding nutritional value.

FOOD FORMS

You can supply your pet with food in three basic forms.

Dry: In this form, the shelf life will be the longest. The concentration of ingredients relative to the total weight of the food will be at its greatest because there will be a low moisture content. This being the case, it means that *it is essential that the hedgehog has free access to water at all times.*

Dry foods for hedgehogs will largely comprise any of the various flavored complete cat diets, those that are now appearing for hedgehogs specifically, or those prepared for ferrets. Feline foods are preferred to those for dogs. They will generally have higher protein and lower carbohydrate content than dog foods. Dry foods are very convenient and are prepared to be nutritionally complete. However, one should apply caution to the last part of the preceding statement: where hedgehogs are concerned, little long-term research has been completed for these animals.

Additionally, the cat and ferret foods are prepared for carnivores, not for animals like the hedgehog, which, in the wild, consumes large quantities of invertebrates. These invertebrates contain chitin, a compound needed by hedgehogs, in their exoskeleton. The notion that these pets can maintain top condition on dry cat foods is incorrect.

Such foods are useful basic diet items, but they must be supplemented with a range of other items to ensure that all required nutrients are being supplied in sufficient variety and quantity to overcome any possibility some may be missing, or not being given in sufficient amounts. The low-cost cat biscuits will contain less proteins than the more costly brands, so stick with those of higher quality.

Moist Foods: These will include commercial canned foods for cats, together with any food item that contains a high-moisture content, such as fresh meats, their byproducts, eggs, fruits, and vegetables. When moist foods are supplied, the pet will drink less water, but it must still be available on a free-choice basis.

Moist foods do not stay fresh for any great length of time. They will spoil quickly if not eaten within a relatively short period of time. Among the foods in this group are beef and other meats, chicken and other poultry, fish, fruits, and vegetables. Be sure that all fresh foods are just that. If you have any doubts, do not feed them to your pet. Meat can be given raw or cooked—a little of both is suggested. It should be cut into small pieces appropriate to the size of the pet.

Chicken should have the skin removed, especially after being cooked. Hedgehogs do not readily digest fats, so be sure only lean meats are given. If not, your pet will soon become obese, with the attendant problems of reducing longevity and possibly creating health problems—the more so for breeding females.

The suggested animal-origin foods are low-fat cottage cheese, gravy stocks poured onto dry food mixtures, and low fat milk. Caution should be applied to milk because it can cause stomach problems if given too often. It need not be given at all to other than hedgehogs that are being hand reared.

Fruits and vegetables form only a very small part of a hedgehog's diet, so do not be overly concerned if yours shows little interest in them. Some of our own stock will eat banana, tomato, apple, strawberry, orange, potato, cauliflower, peas, alfalfa, and boiled rice. These foods are taken

Hedgehogs are capable of picking up scents below the ground to a depth of about an inch or more.

This is a European hedgehog. Its meal consists of a mixture of dry and canned cat foods.

in only small amounts but provide extra vitamins.

Livefoods: Most of the livefoods that these pets would eat in the wild will not be readily available to them under captive conditions. Some owners cannot bring themselves to feed any livefoods to their pets, even if they are only small invertebrates. It is often the handling of such foods rather than the notion of them that puts some pet owners off.

If you are among this group, your pet can survive without livefoods, though for really top condition, and certainly for growing youngsters, some are strongly recommended. The most popular livefood will be mealworms, followed by crickets. The problem with crickets is that they readily escape from open-topped units, but your pet shop may stock wingless insects that will overcome this problem.

Spiders, earthworms, and numerous beetles and their larvae will be taken with various degrees of enthusiasm. Not all invertebrates will be accepted because hedgehogs find some distasteful, and even hedgehogs have taste preferences. You can purchase these foods from your pet store. This is preferable to gathering them in the wild if they are to be a regular part of the diet and also eliminates the risk that they may be carrying the eggs of parasites.

Having said this, if your pet is given some time to roam in your garden under supervision, it will soon find little bugs and beetles to eat, as it will in your home. The risk is probably justified by the obvious benefits to the pet of such exercise and doing what comes very naturally to it— foraging for edible items.

Some hedgehog owners let their pets have supervised "free-time" in the yard or garden. This is fine as long as such areas are not treated with any chemicals.

Establish a regular feeding schedule for your hedgehog and stick to it. The daily rations can be divided into two meals, one served in the morning, the other in the evening.

WHEN AND HOW MUCH TO FEED

Given the nocturnal habits of hedgehogs and your need to observe them as they feed, the best time to supply meals will be in the early evening. Like most animals when it comes to feeding, they are creatures of habit, so it is best to try and feed at the same time each day. However, if you wish to modify their habits so that they will be more active during the day, do this by supplying the main meal at whatever time is most convenient for you. Likewise, you may prefer to feed twice a day, early in the morning and again in the evening. This is probably better for the hedgehog's digestive system.

Divide the rations between the two meals. Additionally to the main meal, you might scatter some dry cat food on the cage floor late at night so that the pet has something to forage for during the night.

The amount to feed is best determined on a trial-and-error basis, which will allow for individual metabolic needs. This is influenced by the activity level of the pet, its age (young animals need extra protein to ensure that they build good muscle), breeding state (sows need more rations when pregnant and feeding their offspring), and general health (pets recovering from illness need more food to compensate for any loss of condition while they were ill).

Supply a varied meal and see how long it takes to be eaten. If it is quickly devoured within five minutes, you have not supplied enough. Give a little more. If the pet eats until it is full, leaving more uneaten than consumed, you can reduce the amount at the next meal. This does assume that the meal contained a number of items that the pet enjoys. The ideal situation is when the hedgehog leaves just a small amount in its dish. This will be consumed somewhat later. Moist foods not eaten within a few hours should be removed and trashed.

A TYPICAL MEAL

Each owner should develop his own range of menus to ensure that all of the major ingredient groups—proteins, fats, carbohydrates, vitamins, and minerals—are supplied in sufficient quantity to achieve maximum growth and health. Further, meals should be such that they do not become boring. Your hedgehog can develop a cosmopolitan appetite only if it is familiar with a range of foods. This makes feeding the pet easier and more interesting. A typical meal may contain a dried cat biscuit (change the flavors periodically), two to four small pieces of meat, two to four mealworms, and one or two pieces

This hedgehog is about to eat a tasty tidbit that it has stumbled upon. In the wild, hedgehogs have the opportunity to eat a wide variety of live foods.

You can offer your hedgehog a variety of different flavored cat foods to see which one is liked most.

each of a fruit and a vegetable. At the next meal, the meat may be replaced by chicken, and a little cottage cheese or scrambled egg added. You may replace the mealworms at another meal with other invertebrates or simply increase the meat or chicken content.

Experiment with mashes that contain a whole range of items all mixed together. This makes it more difficult for the pet to ignore items that you know are nutritious but that are normally rejected if given on their own. Include them in very small amounts so that the pet can develop a taste for them.

PROBLEM EATERS

A number of owners find that on obtaining their pet, it will not eat many of the items discussed in this chapter. The reason is usually because the pet simply has never tasted them, so it ignores them after an initial sniff. This situation usually comes about because the breeder has fed his own stock on a very limited range of foods. The hedgehogs then go to a pet shop, where the diet may be equally as basic. You must introduce new items gradually, small amounts at a time. Withhold whatever they are eating and offer the new food. It must be of the same nutritional

In those countries in which they are indigenous, hedgehogs are welcomed by farmers because they help to keep down the insect population.

The food bowl and the water bottle must be cleaned regularly to prevent the growth of bacteria and other harmful organisms.

value, meaning mealworms or meat in lieu of moist cat or dog food, or these in lieu of mealworms as the case may be.

If the pet steadfastly refuses the new items at that meal, give it its normal foods an hour or so later. Continue with this policy, and over a few days or weeks it should begin to accept the new foods if they are of meat (high-protein types). With respect to fruits and vegetables, it may take longer for their taste to be accepted. In some instances, they may never be, so try a range of them over a period of time.

Few hedgehogs will accept *all* of the various foods that these pets will eat, but *every* hedgehog will eat at least an amount sufficient to ensure that the diet is well balanced. If it fails to, it is usually because the owner has not persevered, because he has not applied ingenuity to widening the diet (mashes, mixes), or because the hedgehog is older than was thought. In the last of the situations just noted, the pet has become accustomed to a

The agouti pattern is the coloration most commonly found in hedgehogs. It is created by the banding of colors—white, black, and brown—on each spine. The agouti coloration can be commonly found in a number of other animals as well.

limited diet and will require much more patience and experimentation to widen its diet. Do bear in mind that it will be more difficult to widen the diet of a pet that is slim and needs little food to maintain its activity level and condition when compared to the heavier pet that has a healthy appetite and is always ready to eat! In the case of the hearty eater, you must ensure that it does not become over-weight, especially if it is not getting sufficient exercise. Never starve your pet if it becomes obese. It can be slimmed down only over a number of months by reducing the quantity at each meal but ensuring that the quality of the meat content is good. If a sow is a poor or finicky eater, it is prudent not to breed her because her offspring will tend to ignore the foods that she ignores. Breed only from very fit sows that will accept a balanced diet, which will be reflected in the quality of their spines, fur, and general demeanor.

This youngster is already accustomed to being handled and is at ease in its owner's hands.

European hedgehog. The agouti coloration of the spines serves as camouflage.

BREEDING

For the most part, hedgehogs are very easy animals to breed. They display few problems, and sows are normally extremely good mothers.

The fact that hedgehogs are potentially quite prolific producers means that they are not in short supply—the situation from just a few years ago having changed dramatically. There is no justification for breeding hedgehogs for its own sake. Pet owners are strongly advised not to do so. Over any term of years, this adversely affects the hobby as a whole.

The following text is written for the person who wishes to become a serious breeder at a low level of participation. This is the ideal way to commence any program. Much of the information will, however, be of value to pet owners presented with an unplanned litter.

THE INITIAL STOCK

If you wish to breed hedgehogs, commence with stock appropriate to your objectives. This means that you should obtain the best that you can afford. The cost of caring for quality animals is no more than the cost of caring for mediocre individuals. Your options are:

1. Obtain a pair or trio of youngsters and rear them to breeding age. This will be the cheapest option. You will be gambling that they mature to be nice hedgehogs, which you cannot be sure of, even if they come from nice parents.
2. Obtain mature youngsters whose quality has been established but whose breeding worth remains unproven.
3. Obtain a boar of proven quality and breeding worth, together with two unrelated females, which may be young and unproven, mature and proven, or one of each.
   The boar is your quality priority because he will be used on both of your females. His potential to spread his

Conditions such as temperature, light, and proper accommodations must be just right before hedgehogs breed and rear their young.

genes, via many matings in a year, is much greater than that of a sow. She can, or should, produce no more than three litters a year. It is this aspect alone that makes him more important to a breeder. From the quality perspective, he can pass no more of his genes to the offspring than can the female. It is best to commence with unrelated females. This gives you two breeding lines. The male can be related to one of the sows. You can compare the progeny of the two lines as they develop.

BREEDING OBJECTIVES

It should never be your objective to breed only for quantity of offspring: this has no merit whatsoever. Your priorities at all times should be:

1. To breed for healthy vigorous stock of excellent temperament. No other criteria is more important. In reality, health and temperament are independent characteristics. You can assess them as such, but give each equal priority over all other considerations.
2. To breed for sound conformation. Never allow size—the desire to produce

larger or smaller than the average—to override the need to retain good type. If you do, it is probable that health will be the first thing that you will have problems with.

Type should always outrank color and pattern, though it is an area in which you may be faced with compromising decisions if you ever breed for the newer color patterns. It doesn't follow that good color always appears in good type, so a degree of balancing may have to be made. But good type is difficult to maintain, good color more readily achieved, so bear this in mind.

3. To retain for onward breeding only those individuals that are at least as good, but preferably better, than one or both of the parents. If none in the litter reach this level, do not retain them; or your quality will steadily deteriorate. Many beginners make this mistake. If subsequent litters with the same parents show no improvement, this tells you that your initial stock is not breeding as good as it looks. One or both parents should be replaced. It would be prudent to mate each parent with other partners to try and establish which of the breeding stock never produces improved youngsters.

BREEDING RECORDS

You cannot conduct a worthwhile program unless you keep detailed records of all matings and their results. They will help you pinpoint problems, as well as being a guide to potential future matings. Records will be of your individual hedgehogs, and breeding records. They should detail such things as which animals were paired, date of mating, date of births, number of offspring, sexes, colors, and any problems along the way and their treatments.

THE MATING AND PREGNANCY

Before any mating is attempted, be very sure that both partners are in top condition. This means neither obese nor very thin. This is especially important in the sow, who must carry and rear the babies. It is also desirable that

she is eating a well-balanced diet: this will encourage the babies to do likewise. Breeding from sows not in top condition may lead to sickly youngsters and mothers who may determine that they cannot rear them, so cannibalize or abandon them.

It is general practice to introduce the female to the male's housing for the purpose of mating. If the female refuses to be mated and attacks the male excessively, she should be removed and placed back with him the following day. If she is not especially aggressive, she can be left with him for 48 hours, when a mating should be assumed to have taken place. She is then placed back with him 12 hours later for an additional day.

Alternatively, if a mating is observed shortly after the first introductions, the sow can be removed and placed back with him 12 hours later. The reason for the repeat mating is that it may maximize litter size, though this has not been established in hedgehogs. Some breeders leave the pair together for a week or more, but in this author's experience this is not necessary.

By the time the babies are about ten days old, it is *usually* safe to handle them. If you are in doubt, wait a few more days.

It may result in the boar unduly pestering the sow.

Once a mating has taken place, the sow is returned to her own housing. The larger this is the better, because it will reduce potential stress when the litter is born. Lack of living space can induce cannibalism in these pets, as can lack of adequate diet. Some early breeders experienced such problems, which were compounded by the fact that they bred mediocre stock that was highly inbred.

Limited inbreeding of itself will normally not produce problems, providing rigorous culling of poor stock is practiced. It is when this is not done that problems may surface. It is beneficial to provide the pregnant female with two nestboxes from which to choose. About two weeks after the litter is born, she may use the vacant box to retire in when wanting to escape the attentions of her growing babies. If for any reason she should become concerned about her babies in the early days after their birth, she may transfer the litter to the other box. This reduces the risk that she will cannibalize them.

BREEDING FACTS

Although you may be told that sows can be bred as young as 12 weeks old, this is poor advice. The youngest recommended age is six months, then only if the female appears to be fully developed physically, and is in excellent condition. We must distinguish between when a sow may be sexually mature (as young as eight weeks old) and when she is physically old enough to cope with birthing and raising a litter.

A youngster should be at least eight weeks old before it goes to its new home. At that age, it should be fully independent of its mother.

The primary goal of a good breeding program is to produce stock that is healthy and of good temperament. Nothing else is more important.

The breeding of very young sows was another reason, beyond those discussed earlier, why cannibalism became associated with these pets. Underage maiden females may easily panic when giving birth and attack their offspring in this stressed state. The average gestation period in hedgehogs is 35 days within a potential range of 34-44 days. Rarely will a litter be produced in days 38-44, but they have been recorded. The litter size potential is one to ten, but three to six would be the average.

Working on the basis of a model 70-75 days from gestation to weaning, it is possible for a sow to produce five litters per year, though four appears to be the maximum. From a breeder's viewpoint, three should be the limit if the sow is to retain full vigor and produce stock of similar condition. She requires ample time between litters to regain her full condition.

The weaning age in these pets ranges from four to eight weeks on average but may extend a few weeks longer if the sow remains with the offspring. It is quite incorrect to assume that all babies are weaned at the same period—be this four, five, or whatever weeks old. Much depends on the size of the litter, the individuals, the foods being received, and environmental factors such as temperature.

With these facts in mind, it is wise to retain youngsters until they are eight weeks old before they go to a new home. At this age, they should be fully independent of their mother and

Dark-eyed white mother and youngster. A calm, even-tempered hedgehog will likely be a better mother than will a nervous one.

ready to go to a new home: a week or two later would actually be even better. The weanlings should be housed in same-sex housing as they reach eight weeks of age.

BIRTHING (PARTURITION)

You will know when the sow is nearing parturition because she will start to put on weight, and her nipples will swell. A few days before the birthing, she will normally start to shore up the entrance to the nestbox with shavings. On the day before and after the births she may show no interest in food or water. Thereafter, she will eat progressively more, so be sure to increase her rations.

At this time, she may become quite belligerent toward you if nest inspection is attempted. Avoid disturbing her until you know from this, and future birthings, how she reacts.

The babies are born blind and helpless in a membrane that shrivels within an hour or so to allow the soft spines to harden. You will hear their squeaks, but avoid the temptation to look. The

Adult female hedgehogs, or sows, are very wary of any disturbances that occur near the nestbox.

sow may become nervous and devour the babies—a quite natural reaction.

The skin of the hoglets is pink; the spines are white. You will see a median spineless tract in the newborns. This is normal for this and most other species. It runs from the head to the tail. As the spines grow, this tract is not seen on the body, and only barely so on the head, once the individual is mature.

Within minutes, the babies are crawling around but are soon gathered by the mother so that they can commence feeding. Their eyes open between days 13 through 16, and they will first start to leave the nest when about 21 days old. By this time they are really adorable.

REARING AND HANDLING

Until the babies start to leave the nest, their nutritional requirements will be supplied via the sow's milk and by food that the mother has regurgitated. It begins their process of familiarization with solid food.

In the following weeks, they will sample all foods offered, especially those eaten by mom. This is the time to supply a good variety so that they do not become accustomed to a narrow range of foods.

With respect to handling, when the sow leaves the nest to eat for the first time after parturition, you can quickly look to see how many babies she has and whether all are healthy. Do not touch them. Any that are dead or have been cannibalized should be removed using a plastic spoon. This is so that your scent is not on the other babies that may have been touched. This could prompt a sow to cannibalize the newborns.

Sometimes a maiden sow will kill one or two babies in panic or error, but thereafter she will rear the rest with no problems. She may kill her entire first litter but be fine in the future. Maybe there is something in her environment that is frightening her—noises, dogs, children disturbing the nest when you are not watching. A sow must be given privacy when having a litter.

By the time the babies are about ten days old, it is *usually* safe to handle them; if you are in doubt, wait a few more days. Once they leave the nest, they should be handled on a daily basis so that they bond to humans and will make fine pets. If this is not done at this time, the youngsters will be much more difficult to socialize as the weeks go by.

Hedgehogs should be handled securely but gently, especially young ones.

Once the hoglets leave the nest, they should be handled on a daily basis so that they bond with humans. This is very important to their becoming good pets.

HANDFEEDING AND FOSTERING

Handfeeding newborn hedgehogs can be done, but it will be a very tiring process on your part. It requires, initially, feedings every two hours, 24 hours a day. It is beyond the scope of this book to discuss the subject in great detail, so you are referred to larger books by this author, and published by TFH Publications. It should be stated, however, that cow's milk should not be used. It can result in the death of the hoglets. Use a milk-substitute formula for kittens.

Fostering can also be successful as long as another female, with hoglets of the same age, can be found. There is always a risk that fostered babies may be rejected, but the alternative may give them no chance at all.

The final comment on breeding is that you should not leave two or more sows in the same housing when one or more give birth. Females have no qualms about devouring the offspring of another hedgehog—a trait not uncommon in many animals. The same applies to a male left with a female at birthing time.

It can seem that breeding these pets is fraught with problems in regard to cannibalism: this is not so, a fact that should be stressed. Most problems arising are likely to be due to human error and interference, or because very nervous females have been bred. Fit, well-socialized, and well-bred females will normally produce litter after litter for you with no problems at all—and may allow nest inspection within days of the birth.

Time for a bedding change. To prevent the growth of pathogens, it is important that bedding be changed on a regular basis.

HEALTH CARE

Hedgehogs are very hardy little animals if given due care in husbandry techniques. Other than being prone to illness if their housing temperature drops suddenly or if it is excessively hot, there are no particular problems presently known to be associated with them, as in dogs or cats, in which distemper and their like are major killer diseases.

However, when a hedgehog does become ill, it is rather more difficult to examine and treat if it is other than a friendly pet. Those sharp little spines can make these matters a prickly and painful affair!

A TYPICAL MAMMAL

One problem that hedgehog owners have encountered is that many vets are loathe to attempt diagnosis or treatment of these pets because they are unfamiliar with them. As a consequence, the NAHA receives hundreds of telephone calls from worried owners looking for instant diagnosis and treatment recommendations based on the symptoms they describe.

It is not possible to render either service to owners via a telephone. If your pet shows signs of illness, you *must* take it to a small animal vet and request that

When you handle your pet, check the condition of the spines. A dense coat of spines usually is indicative of healthy skin.

he treat it as a typical small mammal with respect to diagnostic techniques and treatments. As with any other pet, dosage of drugs should be based on weight. It is true that hedgehogs do possess a high resistance to certain toxins, but it is also true that they respond to modern drugs much as does any other animal of their size and weight. It must be added that the limited information available to vets does mean that some will be reluctant to treat a hedgehog without known protocols. However, in such instances, try to find a vet who will work with you. Do accept that there is an element of the unknown with these pets. Tell your vet you accept this reality. An attempt at diagnosis and treatment is better than none! It is the only way the boundaries of our knowledge about these pets can be expanded.

PREVENTIVE MEDICINE

Given the present situation with hedgehogs, avoiding problems has to be your best health care policy, so a quick review of hygiene factors is appropriate.

1. A cage home needs cleaning daily—water pots, food containers, and removal of any soiled floor covering. Each week it will need a complete cleaning, including the nestbox. With a nursing mother, you need to keep the food vessels clean, and gather fecal matter, but do minimal

Preventing problems before they can get a chance to start is the best health care policy for your hedgehog.

A good example of hedgehog housing that is obviously well maintained. Remember that everything in the cage—including decorative wooden items—must be cleaned regularly.

tidying of the rest of the housing for the first two weeks after the offspring are born so as not to unduly disturb them. Be sure to clean the cage bars. Your pet will rub its snout on them. Pathogens and parasites can gain entry to the mouth and facial fur from this action.

2. Furnishings, such as logs and rocks, should be scrubbed and rinsed each week if they are kept in housing with limited space. They will survive rather longer in large habitat housing.

3. Replace any cracked or chipped water or food vessels.

4. Remove soiled floor covering each day. Keep fresh floor covering materials in a suitably sealed container.

5. Always wash your hands before and after handling each pet. Direct transfer from one place to another is a common method by which pathogens travel.

6. Keep all foods in sealed containers, especially in a breeding room. Floors and all surfaces should be kept free of dust and dirt.

7. Keep your eye on the temperature during the winter months. In the wild, hedgehogs are conditioned to a more variable range of temperatures, which they are able to well cope with. Under captive conditions, the more stable temperature of a home or breeding room means that sudden frosts in non-regulated

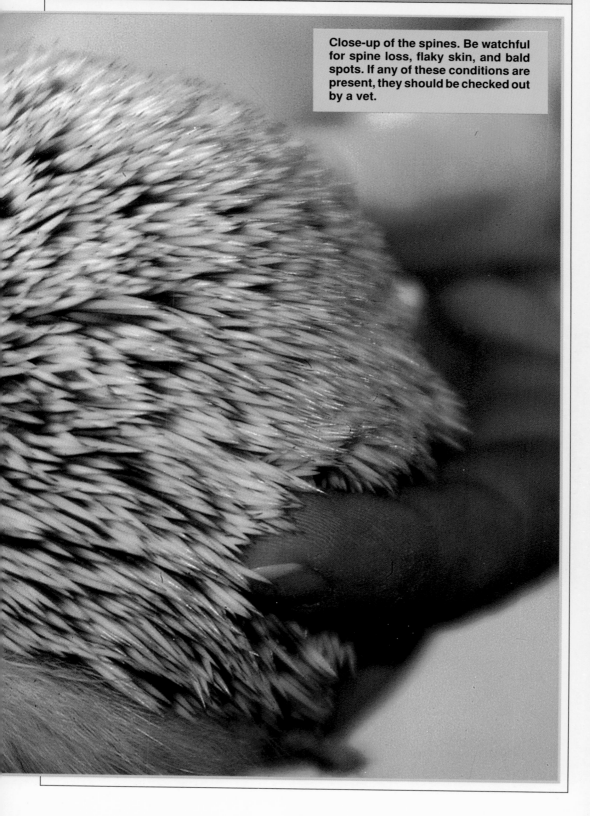

Close-up of the spines. Be watchful for spine loss, flaky skin, and bald spots. If any of these conditions are present, they should be checked out by a vet.

rooms can quickly induce a chill and torpid state in a pet. At such a time, the pet is generally more susceptible to parasites and pathogens.

8. Whenever you are handling your pet, take the opportunity to carefully examine its soft fur and the base of the spines. Brush them against their lie with your hand, at which time any parasites will be visible. Look also for any sores, or bald areas, which would indicate parasitic action. Wipe these areas with an antiseptic lotion.

If the bald areas have whorls, this suggests ringworm, a fungal parasite that will need veterinary attention to confirm and treat. A powdery dust at the base of the spines indicates mite attack—the spines will eventually start to fall out.

Most problems arise due to a breakdown in hygiene that allows pathogenic colonization. The effect intensifies if the diet is inadequate, if the pet is stressed, and/or if the temperature moves below or above the comfort zone.

STRESS

Stress is a subconscious condition which reduces the hedgehog's immune system from working as effectively as it should. It increases susceptibility to illness. It may of itself create problems in the form of syndromes.

They include eating fecal matter, wood chewing, self mutilation, cannibalism, abandonment of young, pacing, overt aggression, and excessive eating and drinking. Each of these has an alternative source, which makes diagnosing the condition difficult.

It has been established in other animals that the more natural the situation denied the individual, the greater the stress factor. For example, all animals need a given amount of space in which to live. If their house is too small, they will become stressed. Hedgehogs are foraging animals: if they cannot do this, it will stress them.

If their diet is too restrictive, it will create stress. If their house is not supplied with a nestbox or other place of hiding, this too will induce the condition. Children or other pets that continually disturb a hedgehog, especially when it is sleeping, will increase the stress factor.

Because it is difficult to pinpoint stress as the reason for a given problem or illness, it is best to ensure that the conditions discussed as being stressors are avoided. If you are a pet owner who has just been blessed with an unwanted litter and the mother has killed one or more of her babies, do ensure that stress is not likely to be a problem. If it is, rectify the situation *immediately*. It may reduce her tension so that the rest of the litter are nursed.

DIAGNOSING ILLNESS

There are two ways that your pet will indicate that it is unwell. One is by changes in its behavior pattern, the other will be via clinical signs. Often, behavior changes are the first indicators: sometimes they may be the only clues to an unwell pet.

Behavioral Indicators

You will be aware of these only if you spend much time observing your hedgehog.

1. Is it eating less than its normal amount of food, and is it showing reduced enthusiasm for favored tidbits?
2. Is it spending more time than usual sleeping?
3. Is it displaying any behavioral signs that are not normal for it?

Clinical Indicators:

You are not advised to attempt home diagnosis of any but the most minor of problems. Clinical signs for most diseases and conditions are much the same. Even your vet will need to analyze skin scrapings, as well as blood and fecal samples, in order to determine the problem, its likely cause, and the best treatment.

The following indicate a problem, the more so if they persist beyond 24 hours and are in association with each other: running nose or eyes, labored breathing, excessive scratching,

The more familiar you are with your hedgehog's behavior, the better able you will be to discern when it is not well.

4. Does it seem reluctant to be handled when this has never been a problem?
5. Is it displaying a much reduced activity level?

If the answer to any of these questions is "yes," you should note the time of day and then inspect the pet very carefully for body swellings, abdominal hardness, or any other malevolent clinical signs. If the pet is clearly distressed, or in pain, contact your vet immediately.

diarrhea, swellings, blood-streaked fecal matter, vomiting, coughing, skin abrasions, loss of spines, bald spots, flaky encrustations on the face or body fur, powdery dust at base of spines, involuntary muscle twitching, and inability to walk in a normal manner. Note when they were first observed and if they have gotten worse, and over what time period. Now consult your vet. If the signs are those such as a minor discharge from the eyes and/or nose, this may be symptomatic of a chill and should respond within 24 hours to extra heat in a draft-free room. Likewise, a minor abdominal problem from overeating or a change in the diet may result in diarrhea. It should not persist beyond 24-36 hours. Withhold moist foods for 12-24 hours, but maintain the water supply.

Always bear in mind that the longer you wait to contact your vet, the more time the problem has to develop if it is more than a minor condition. This is a judgment call that can be made based only on the situation and signs discussed.

WHAT TO DO

Having decided that the pet is unwell, your first reaction must be to isolate it from all other pets. Take a few moments to write down the clinical signs. Note the state of its most recent bowel movement, and, ideally, gather a few samples. Note the temperature of the room in which the pet is living. Has it changed dramatically over the last 24 hours? If it has, this could induce a torpid state that will be overcome by increasing the temperature. The housing should now be thoroughly cleaned. If the condition does not show improvement within 12 hours, it would be wise to consult your vet.

EXTERNAL PARASITES

Mites, fleas, and ticks are the three possible external parasites that could invade your hedgehog. Mites are slow-moving critters;

whereas fleas will be seen to scurry quickly if the fur is disturbed on inspection. However, it is probable that any fleas on your pet will be temporary residents that have come from another pet—dog, cat, rabbit— and will not stay long. (Many of these parasites are species specific.) Ectoparasites can be eradicated using an insecticide from your veterinarian. A word of caution is appropriate: it has been noted that those insecticides containing N-octyl bicycloheptene dicarboxamide, when combined with pyrethrins, may prove dangerous, even fatal, to these pets. Labels should therefore be scrutinized.

It is also wise to use only one ectoparasiticide at a time. For example, do not use one on the pet and another brand on its housing. You cannot assess possible side effects if this is done, and it may duplicate toxins that may be deleterious to the pet.

If your hedgehog reacts adversely to insecticides or any other topical (applied to the skin) treatment, this should be removed by spraying with tepid water or dipping the pet into a shallow bowl. (The second method is best.) Be sure water does not get into the eyes or ears. Allergic reactions may evidence themselves in the form of involuntary twitching, vomiting, or breathing difficulties. Consult your vet if this should happen.

INTERNAL PARASITES

All pets can suffer from worm infestations of numerous kinds.

These worms include roundworm, tapeworm, heartworm, lung, and liver worms. Emaciation, dry skin, loss of spines, vomiting, loss of appetite, diarrhea, and blood-streaked fecal matter are clinical signs. In some instances, such as those that invade the organs, there may be no obvious physical signs. Only autopsy reveals their presence.

Periodic egg counts by your vet will establish what level of worms are present. It is wise to routinely deworm breeding sows some weeks prior to mating. It is also wise not to presume which worms are causing a problem and treat the condition yourself just to avoid a vet bill.

FUNGAL PROBLEMS

Fungi are primitive plants that do not form chlorophyll. A large number of them survive as parasites on living tissue. One is known as ringworm and forms whorls on the skin, which is reddened and flaky where the lesion is created. Fungi may also infect the respiratory tract, the digestive system, and the reproductive tract. Identification of fungi is essential before treatment is attempted, so again you must consult your vet if ringworm, in particular, is suspected. It can be transferred to humans. Fungi survive best where conditions are dirty: stagnant water, moldy vegetation

All hedgehogs need a safe, secure retreat.

(piles of grass cuttings and their like), and in the soil. After gardening, always wash your hands before handling your pets—ideally, wear appropriate gardening gloves as well.

COAT CONDITIONERS

A number of owners, upon noticing that the skin of their pets is dry, or the spines shedding, seek advice as to what coat conditioners they can apply to remedy the situation. The answer is none. Your hedgehog's skin, fur, and spines grow, and are nourished, from within. The application of external lotions may at best mask dryness but will not overcome the underlying problem(s).

This will be related to the diet, an internal problem, or the action of external parasites. Identify and overcome this, and the coat will be healthy, the spines "springy."

Maintaining your hedgehog in fine health is all about providing roomy housing, keeping all things clean at all times, and ensuring that the diet is wholesome. Attend to these matters, and you will be unlikely, and unlucky, to need veterinary attention. If you suspect this may be appropriate, solicit it sooner rather than later, when treatment may not be effective and will be more costly.

Doting mom and youngster. Hedgehogs are hardy animals if given due care in husbandry techniques.

THE NORTH AMERICAN HEDGEHOG ASSOCIATION (NAHA)

Since its formation in the Spring of 1993, the NAHA has proved invaluable in helping to stabilize the hedgehog hobby. It was the first association in the world to be devoted to hedgehogs kept as pets in a domestic environment. Possibly more than in any other area, its impact has been in helping beginners with their problems. It has also advised many institutions and other professional bodies on various aspects of these pets. The association has been the administrative center that has gathered and disseminated information to any person requiring information about these pets. It has been instrumental in helping to fight restrictive legislation in numerous states where these pets were illegal. It publishes an excellent glossy magazine called *Hedgehog World International* (formerly *The Hedgehog News*), which carries a range of articles for hobbyists.

During 1995, the NAHA appointed a national panel of breeder experts as judges to draw up a standard of excellence for these pets in readiness for exhibitions that will begin in 1996. You may be a subscriber to the magazine, or an active member of the association. As a member of the association, you may register your breeding affix, your stock, and their pedigrees.

All enthusiasts are strongly recommended to support the NAHA, not only for the untiring work it has already done, but also in order to further its objective of providing hobbyists with a central body to represent and administrate the best interests of all involved with these pets—and especially the welfare of the hedgehogs themselves.

You do not need to live in the US to be a member. The NAHA has, and welcomes, enthusiasts from any country in which these animals are admired and/or kept.

One area the association *cannot* give you advice on is related to diagnosis and treatment of illnesses. Hundreds of worried owners telephone the NAHA seeking such information. Other than general comments, the officers of the association will *not* attempt to give you any more advice than is already in this book. Veterinarians are the *only* people qualified to do this.

Should you wish to obtain more information on the NAHA, it issues an information packet, and its address is given herewith. Please bear in mind time differences when telephoning the association, which operates normal office hours Monday through Friday, Mountain Standard Time.

NAHA
PO Box 122
Nogal, New Mexico 88341
USA
Telephone: 1-505-648-2835

In the wild, hedgehogs will seek shelter during the hot hours of the day.